337
c

599
.7357
BAI

MW00954809

Animal World

Giraffes

Donna Bailey

STECK-VAUGHN
LIBRARY
A Division of Steck-Vaughn Company

Did you know that a giraffe is
the tallest animal in the world?
Most adult male giraffes are about
18 feet tall, although the tallest
can be 20 feet tall.

Giraffes live in herds in
the grasslands of Africa.
Their long legs and long neck
let them eat the leaves at the top
of their favorite trees.

The patterns on a giraffe's body
help it hide from its enemies.
Masai giraffes have an uneven pattern
of blotches, which helps them hide
in the shade of the trees.

4

A reticulated giraffe has
a regular pattern of even shapes
separated by thin, white lines.
This reticulated giraffe is swishing
its tufted tail to keep away the flies.

A giraffe has three skin-covered horns—
two on top of its head and
one between its eyes.
Its large eyes can see things a long way off.
A giraffe can hear well, too, and turns
its ears to catch the slightest sound.

A giraffe's hairy, rubbery lips nibble at the branches of the most prickly thorns. Its long tongue stretches out to reach the leaves at the top of the tree.

The giraffe has a short mane down
the back of its neck.
Its long neck has only seven bones,
just like you have in your neck.
Of course, the bones in a giraffe's neck
are much larger than your neck bones.

If attacked by a lion, a giraffe defends
itself by kicking with its heavy hoofs.
When two male giraffes fight,
they don't kick each other.
The giraffe swings its long neck back, then
smashes it against the other giraffe's
neck with a loud thud.

A giraffe spreads its legs wide to reach
the water when it drinks.
It would be easy for a lion to attack
a giraffe standing in this position.
One giraffe always keeps watch when
the others in the herd are drinking.

10

Giraffes always keep a lookout.
A herd usually stands facing in
different directions to see all around.
Giraffes are so tall and can see so far
that other animals, such as these zebra,
stay near a giraffe herd.

If a giraffe sees a danger, it warns the other giraffes in the herd and they all run off. When a giraffe runs, both hind legs move together and both front legs move together. A galloping giraffe can go as fast as 35 miles an hour.

A giraffe ambles when it walks.
First it lifts its left legs off
the ground and then its right legs.
Its neck swings backward and forward
to help it balance as it walks.

Giraffes usually sleep standing up.
Their long legs and big body make it
hard for them to get up quickly if a lion
is nearby.
When they rest on the ground, they close
their eyes only for a few minutes.

Giraffes lick each other
to keep each other clean.
They also rub up against trees
to get rid of old skin and fur.

Can you see the little oxpecker bird
sitting on this giraffe's back?
The little bird picks off fleas, dirt,
and ticks from the giraffe's skin.

A herd of giraffes usually has
between ten and twenty females
and some young giraffes.
There may be one or two adult males.
Males don't usually stay with the herd
for long.

Male giraffes are called bulls.

Bulls are bigger and heavier than females.

A bull lives on his own most of the time.

He spends his time eating and
looking for a mate.

Female giraffes are called cows.
When a cow is five years old,
she is ready to mate with a bull.
She will have about seven to nine babies
during her life.

About 14 months after the cow and
the bull mate, the baby giraffe is born.
The mother finds a quiet place
where she can give birth.

The mother stands up during the birth.
The baby giraffe's front legs
come out first and then its head.
The baby falls six feet to the ground.
A newborn baby is about six feet tall
and weighs about 110 pounds.

The baby giraffe lies in the grass and rests for a while.

The mother licks her newborn calf and makes it clean.

About an hour after its birth,
the baby calf tries to stand up.
It is very wobbly as it gets up
on its long legs.

The mother giraffe stays close to her baby.
The calf soon learns to drink
its mother's milk.

For the first six weeks, the young calf
stays near its mother.
Later it may wander off, but it runs back
to hide under her when it is afraid.

The mother sometimes leaves her calf
in a nursery with other calves.
While their mothers go off to look
for food, the calves are watched over
by two other females.

After two or three months, the calf
learns to nibble leaves.
The calf drinks its mother's milk
until it is nine or ten months old.

The young giraffe stays with the herd
until it is fully grown.
When they are fully grown, the males leave
the herd and live on their own.

A giraffe spends most of the day
nibbling the leaves of bushes and trees.
It swallows its food quickly before
it has chewed the food completely.

Later on, the giraffe will chew the cud,
the way a cow does.
It finds a place safe from danger
and brings lumps of food from
its stomach up its long neck.

The giraffe grinds the food with
its strong back teeth.
When the food is well chewed and
has turned into a thin liquid,
the giraffe swallows it again.

Giraffes also need salt to keep healthy.
They find salt licks where they can lick
the salty soil.
They also swallow lumps of the soil.
Other animals, such as this warthog,
join them at the salt lick.

Index

Editorial Consultant: Donna Bailey
Executive Editor: Elizabeth Strauss
Project Editor: Becky Ward

Picture research by Jennifer Garratt
Designed by Richard Garratt Design

33<.>
Forest Hill Public School
LIBRARY
TORONTO BOARD OF EDUCATION
20237

Photographs
Cover: Bruce Coleman (Norman Myers)
Bruce Coleman: 4 (M. P. Kahu); 5, 14, 17 (Hans Reinhard); 6 (K. Wothe); 7 (Gunter Ziesler); 8, 13, 19 (Mark Boulton); 9 (Masud Gureshi); 11 (Frans Lanting); 12 (J & D Bartlett); 15, 28 (Peter Davey); 18 (G. Langsbury); 20, 25, 27 (Jeff Foott); 29 (Kim Taylor); 31 (Rod Williams); 32 (Jane Burton)
OSF Picture Library: title page (R. Packwood); 2 (Warwick Johnson); 3 (S. A. Sabi-Sand); 10 (Patti Murray); 16 (Stan Osolinski); 21, 22, 23, 24 (R. Ben Shahar); 26 (David Cayless); 30 (M & B Reed)

Library of Congress Cataloging-in-Publication Data: Bailey, Donna. Giraffes / Donna Bailey. p. cm.— (Animal world) Includes index. SUMMARY: Studies the physical characteristics, behavior, and life cycle of the world's tallest animal. ISBN 0-8114-2646-7 1. Giraffes—Juvenile literature. [1. Giraffes.] I. Title. II. Series: Animal world (Austin, Tex.) QL737.U56B35 1991 599.73′57—dc20 90-22108 CIP AC

ISBN 0-8114-2646-7
Copyright 1991 Steck-Vaughn Company
Original copyright Heinemann Children's Reference 1991

All rights reserved. No part of the material protected by this copyright may be reproduced or utilized in any form or by any means, electronic or mechanical, including photocopying, recording, or by any information storage and retrieval system, without permission in writing from the copyright owner. Requests for permission to make copies of any part of the work should be mailed to: Copyright Permissions, Steck-Vaughn Company, P.O. Box 26015, Austin, Texas 78755. Printed in the United States of America.

1 2 3 4 5 6 7 8 9 0 LB 96 95 94 93 92 91